Highlights

AGES 6–7

Hands-On STEAM
Learning Fun Workbook

For information about permission to reproduce selections from this book for
an entire school or school district, please contact permissions@highlights.com.

Published by Highlights Learning • 815 Church Street • Honesdale, Pennsylvania 18431
ISBN: 978-1-64472-296-1
Mfg. 11/2020
Printed in Madison, WI, USA
First edition
10 9 8 7 6 5 4 3 2 1

For assistance in the preparation of this book, the editors would like to thank:
Vanessa Maldonado, MSEd; MS Literacy Ed. K–12; Reading/LA Consultant Cert.; K–5 Literacy Instructional Coach
Kristin Ward, MS Curriculum, Instruction, and Assessment; K–5 Mathematics Instructional Coach
Jump Start Press, Inc.

Sounds All Around

Sound is energy made by vibrations. **Vibrations** are quick movements back and forth. Some vibrations you can see. Some you cannot.

What sounds might you hear at this football game? Circle each person or thing that is making a sound. Then tell about the silly things you see.

Hold your hand on your throat as you talk. Can you feel the vibrations?

TALK ABOUT IT!

- Close your eyes. Listen to the sounds around you. What do you hear?
- What sounds can you make with your mouth? With your hands? With your feet?

Investigate:
Quiet or Loud

What are some objects or animals that are quiet? What are some objects or animals that are loud?

YOU NEED:
- rubber band
- paper or plastic cup

1. Stretch the rubber band over your thumb and pointer finger. Pluck the band. Watch it vibrate. Listen for the sound.

2. Now, place the cup on its side. Put your hand in front of the opening. Pluck the rubber band again. What do you notice?

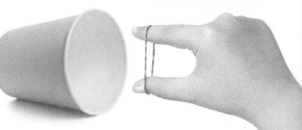

What is the girl using to make her voice louder? Draw a box around it. Then find the **9** objects in this Hidden Pictures puzzle.

 flashlight

crescent moon

 ring

 frog

 envelope

 ruler

 baseball bat

 glove

 fried egg

Investigate:
Dancing Rice

Sound travels in waves. Sound waves can make glass and other materials vibrate.

🔍 How can you "see" sound?

YOU NEED:
- plastic wrap
- large bowl
- large rubber band
- 1 tablespoon uncooked rice
- portable speaker or music player

1. Place a long piece of plastic wrap over the top of the bowl. Pull it tight. Use the rubber band to hold the wrap in place.
2. Put the rice on top of the plastic wrap.
3. Hold the speaker up next to the bowl. Play loud music!
4. Watch the rice.

TALK ABOUT IT!
- What happens to the rice on the plastic wrap?
- What does this investigation show you?

TEST IT AGAIN
- Change the volume. What happens when you play the music quietly or more loudly?
- Change the type of music. Does the beat of the music affect how the rice moves?
- Try different materials, such as salt or crumpled pieces of paper. How do those objects move?

 # Invent:
A Musical Instrument

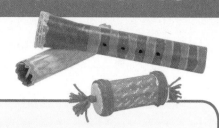

Design and build a musical instrument.
What will it look like? How will it make sound?

YOU NEED:

- materials to make an instrument base, such as an empty tissue box or cardboard tube
- materials to play the instrument, such as string, rubber bands, uncooked rice, or straws
- paper • scissors • tape or glue • markers or paint

NOTE: You may need to ask an adult to cut a hole or holes in the base.

1. Draw a design of your instrument.
2. Choose the materials. Start with the base. Cut a hole and add strings, if you want. Add other materials, such as small straws if you will blow into the instrument, or rice if it's a shaker.
3. Use markers or paint to decorate your instrument.
4. Play your instrument to test it.

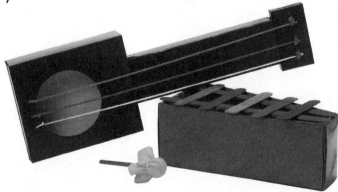

EVALUATE AND REDESIGN

- How well did your instrument work?
- What could you change to make the instrument sound better?
- Try out different designs. Compare the results.

What Is Light?

How does the daytime sky look different from the nighttime sky? In the day, light from the sun makes the sky bright. **Light** is energy that lets you see.

All the pictures below show light. Circle each light that is from nature. Cross off each light that is made by people.

sun

fireworks

flashlight

lamp

fire

firefly

TALK ABOUT IT!
- How is the light in all the pictures the same? How is it different?
- What else gives off light?

 # Investigate:
Pinhole Boxes

🔍 **Why do we need light?**

YOU NEED:
- 3 small objects, such as a toy, a cup, and a sock
- 3 cardboard boxes
- packing tape • pen • flashlight

1. Ask an adult to be your helper. Have your helper get 3 small objects without showing you what they are.

2. Ask your helper to place each object in a box and seal it with tape.

3. Use a pen to poke a small hole in the side of each box.

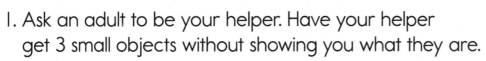

4. Look through each hole. What do you see? Record it in the **No Flashlight** column in the chart.

5. Poke another hole in the top of each box. Have your helper shine the flashlight in the top hole as you look through the side hole.

6. Now what do you see? Record it in the **Flashlight** column.

	No Flashlight	Flashlight
BOX 1		
BOX 2		
BOX 3		

TALK ABOUT IT!
- At first, what did the inside of each box look like?
- How did the flashlight help you?
- What did this investigation show about light?

Shadow Play

Light travels in a straight line. Some materials allow light to pass through them. Some materials block light.

These hands are making shadow puppets. Draw a line from each set of hands to the shadow it makes.

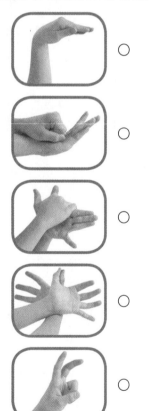

TRY THIS!

Have someone hold up a flashlight. Put your hands between the light and a wall and try making each of the shadow puppets above. Have fun moving your hands! Look at how the shadows change.

Create: Candle Holder

This nature scene is not outside the window. It *is* the window—a stained-glass window. Artists use a special process to "stain" colored scenes into glass.

Stained glass is translucent. It lets some light pass through it.

Make your own stained glass!

YOU NEED:

- colored tissue paper
- paint brush
- white glue
- glass jar
- battery-powered candles

1. Cut or tear tissue paper into small pieces.
2. With a paint brush, put glue on a small part of the jar. Cover the glue with tissue paper.
3. Repeat until you have covered the outside of the jar.
4. Turn on a battery-powered candle. Drop it in the jar. Watch your stained-glass jar glow.

TALK ABOUT IT!

- What color tissue paper did you use? Do different colors affect how much light shines through?
- What other objects might be made with stained glass?

Light

🔍 How much light passes through different materials?

Light can pass through some materials, but not others. Materials that let all light through are transparent. Materials that block light are opaque.

YOU NEED:
- clear bottle • flashlight
- crayons or markers
- waxed paper • cardboard

1. Make a prediction: circle the object you think will allow the most light to pass through.

2. In a dark room, hold the bottle in one hand so your fingers are behind it.

3. With your other hand, aim the flashlight at the bottle.

4. How much light passes through the bottle? Where do you see the light beam? Can you see your fingers behind the bottle? Use the chart to record what you see.

5. Repeat steps 2–4 with the waxed paper and the cardboard.

Clear Bottle	Waxed Paper	Cardboard

TALK ABOUT IT!

- Think about your prediction. Was it correct? How do you know?
- What other items could you test?

Investigate:
Reflected Light

Hold a metal spoon in front of you. Can you see yourself in it? A smooth, shiny object can **reflect** light.

Light that reflects off a surface bounces back.

 How does a mirror reflect light?

> **YOU NEED:**
> • handheld mirror • flashlight

1. Hold the mirror. Aim the flashlight at the mirror. Where does the light go?
2. Move the flashlight and mirror to test different directions.
   • Shine the light from the left and from the right.
   • Hold the mirror facing up. Shine the light down on it.
   • Hold the mirror facing down. Shine the light up at it.
3. Look to see where the light beams move when the light and mirror move.

> **TALK ABOUT IT!**
> • Is there a pattern to where the light beams move?
> • What other objects have a smooth, shiny surface? How could you test how they reflect light?

TRY THIS!

A **mirror ball** is covered with small mirrors. When the ball turns, it reflects light in many directions. Try making your own mirror ball with household objects, such as a small ball and aluminum foil.

Devices From Here to There

How do people send messages to each other when they are apart? Years ago, people often wrote letters. Today, people have many more choices for sending messages.

Look at the photo and the big picture. Name the things that can be used to send messages. Then find the **12** objects in this Hidden Pictures puzzle.

 mushroom

 ladybug

 oven mitt

 comb

 sailboat

 belt buckle

 envelope

 clothespin

 bandage

 ice-cream pop

 teapot

 flashlight

People may use emojis in their messages. What does each of these emojis mean?

TALK ABOUT IT!
- What things do you use to send messages? How do you use them?
- How has the way people send messages changed from the past? How is it the same?

Investigate:
Sound Messages

Sound waves travel faster through solids than they do through air.

Ask a friend to stand across the room and whisper to you. How well can you hear what was said?

🔍 **How can you use a paper-cup telephone to hear better?**

YOU NEED:
- pencil   • 2 paper cups
- 36-inch-long string or yarn   • tape

1. Use a pencil to poke a small hole in the bottom of each cup.

2. Push the ends of the string through the holes. Knot the ends of the string. Tape each knot to the inside of a cup.

3. Hold one cup. Have a friend hold the other cup. Stand apart. Pull on the string to stretch it tight.

4. Take turns talking into the cups. Hold the cup in front of your mouth to talk. Hold the cup next to your ear to listen to the other person.

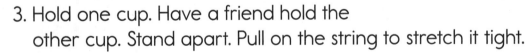

TALK ABOUT IT!
- How well could you hear with the cups? Was it better or worse than without the cups?
- Try another object to speak in to, such as an empty wrapping-paper roll. How does the sound of your voice change?

 Invent:

Light Messages

People can use light to send messages. Look at these lights. How does each one send a message?

How can you use light to send messages?

Invent a way to send messages with light. What materials will you need? How will your invention work?

Make a plan. Draw and label pictures to show your plan. Think about these questions:

- What will you use for light—a flashlight? A glow stick? Something else?
- How will you send messages? Will you use flashes or colored lights? What else could you do?

Now follow your plan to make your invention!

TALK ABOUT IT!
- Tell about your invention. How does it work?
- What problems did you have? How could you solve those problems?

Animal Eyes

Many animals have special eyes. Their eyes help them get the information they need to live. For example, frogs can see color at night, which is when they hunt. And an eagle's vision is so sharp it can see a bug crawling on the ground from a perch in a tall tree!

I spy . . . an animal's eye! But what kind of animal? Write an animal name from the box on the line next to the correct eye.

| cat | hawk | hermit crab | iguana |

 _____

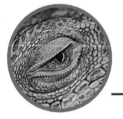 _____

 _____

 _____

TALK ABOUT IT!

• What color are your eyes? How do you use them? What can you learn by using your eyes?

• Close your eyes and try to (safely) move around your home. What is it like to move without seeing?

Animal Safety

Animals try to stay safe from predators. Predators are other animals that might eat them.

An animal's body parts can help it stay safe. Some animals have shells. Some animals have sharp claws or quills. Other animals have body coverings that blend in with what is around them.

Draw a line from each body part to the animal it belongs to.

quills ○

a shell ○

covering that blends in ○

TALK ABOUT IT!

• What other animals have shells? How can a shell help an animal stay safe?

• How does blending in help an animal stay safe?

• What are other body parts that can help animals stay safe?

Animal Movements

Animals have body parts that help them move in different ways.

Move like Australian animals.
Do this action rhyme!

I slither on my belly like a
king brown snake.

Push up! I'm a gecko,
chirping as I wake.

Next, I'm a fairy penguin,
waddling to the sea.

Jump up! I'm a wallaby,
hopping and free.

TALK ABOUT IT!
- How does the shape of a snake's body help it slither?
- Which body part must be strong for an animal to hop?

Investigate:
Neighborhood Birds

✂ **Make a telescope to watch birds!**

YOU NEED:

- cardstock
- cardboard tube
- rubber bands
- art materials for decorating (stickers, crayons, markers)

1. Roll a piece of cardstock over a cardboard tube. Add some rubber bands.
2. Decorate your telescope.
3. Pull the tube to make your telescope longer.
4. Look for birds outside. What are they doing? What body parts are they using?
5. In the box below, draw a bird you see. Write to tell about how it uses its body parts.

A bird's **beak** helps it eat its food.

A blue jay's pointy beak helps it eat berries.

A heron's long, sharp beak helps it catch fish.

TALK ABOUT IT!

What birds did you see? How were the parts of different birds alike? How were they different?

Plant Parts

Plants have parts that help them live and grow.

Read each label below. Draw a line from the label to the plant part it matches.

A **leaf** takes in sunlight.

The **stem** helps water move up from the roots to other parts of the plant.

Roots take in water from the ground.

A plant sprouts from a **seed**.

Some plants have flowers and fruits. A flower makes seeds. A fruit holds seeds.

TALK ABOUT IT!

- Which part do you think best helps a plant stay in the ground?
- What types of plants have you seen near your home?
- How are the parts of different types of plants alike? How are they different?

Plant Growth

Plants need sunlight, water, air, and space to grow.

Do this action rhyme to show how a seedling grows.

I'm a little seedling
sleeping on the ground.

I reach for the sun,
but I don't make a sound.

I open up my leaves
when the raindrops fall.

Rain helps me grow up
straight and tall!

TALK ABOUT IT!
- How does a plant "reach for the sun"?
- Why do you think raindrops help a plant to grow?

Ideas from Nature

Look at that beak! It helps the kingfisher dive into water without much of a splash.

Engineers studied the kingfisher's beak. They used its shape to design the front of a high-speed train. One way this shape helps the train is by allowing it to speed through tunnels without making much sound.

Some engineers mimic, or copy, ideas from nature to solve problems.

Draw a line from each invention to the plant or animal it copies.

TALK ABOUT IT!

- Some animals have sticky pads on their feet. The pads help them walk up walls. What might you invent using that idea?

- What are some other plants or animals that might give people ideas for inventions?

Invent:
A Listening Device

Inventions are designed to solve problems. Which of these inventions have you used? What problems do they solve? Do you think any mimic an idea from nature?

How can you listen to quiet sounds?

Have you ever tried to listen carefully in a noisy place? Imagine you want to hear sounds that are very quiet. Use an idea from nature to help you design a listening invention.

Draw and label pictures to plan your invention. Include the following information:

- What idea from nature will you copy?
- What will you use to make your invention?
- How will you keep the invention near your ears?
- How will it work?

This fox can hear sounds from far away. What do you notice about its ears? Cup your hands behind your ears. Can you hear sounds better?

TALK ABOUT IT!
Tell about your invention. How does it copy an idea from nature?

Animals and Their Young

This is an adult boar and its young. How are they the same? How are they different?

Look at each adult animal and its young. Write one way they are the same. Write one way they are different.

	Same	Different

TALK ABOUT IT!
- Look at each young animal on this page. How do you think each one will look as an adult? Why do you think so?
- Do all young animals look similar to an adult?
- Think about baby frogs. Do tadpoles look the same as an adult frog? How are they different?

Adult and Young Animals

Draw a line to match each adult animal on the left with its young on the right.

TALK ABOUT IT!
- How could you tell which young animal matches each adult animal?
- Have you ever seen a young animal? What did it look like?

Animal Babies

Look at each animal listed in the clue box. Write the name of the animal's baby in the crossword puzzle. Use the word box to help. We did one to get you started.

CLUE BOX

ACROSS	DOWN
1. ~~cow~~	2. deer
3. cat	3. goat
4. dog	4. pig
5. duck	6. hen
8. bear	7. sheep

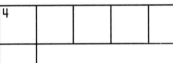

¹CALF²

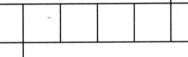

(Crossword grid with numbered squares: 1 across CALF, 3 across, 4 across, 5 across, 6 down, 7 down, 8 down)

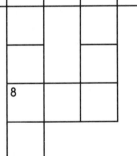
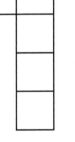

WORD BOX

~~calf~~	kid
chick	kitten
cub	lamb
duckling	piglet
fawn	puppy

TALK ABOUT IT!
- Where might you see a baby cow or a baby goat? Where might you see a baby dog or a baby cat?
- What other animal babies do you know?

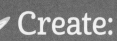

Create:
Animal Families

Choose 2 kinds of animals. Make cardboard figures to show each animal and its young.

> **YOU NEED:**
> • scissors • cardboard • glue • colored paper • fabric

1. Have an adult help you cut cardboard into big rectangles, small squares, and long rectangles.

2. Glue the cardboard pieces together to make animal shapes.

3. Glue small pieces of colored paper and fabric to your animals to make body coverings.

4. Use the figures to tell about each animal and its young.

Make sure your figures show how young animals and their parents are alike and different.

TALK ABOUT IT!
• What animals did you choose?
• How did you use the materials to show differences between the parents and their young?

Protecting Their Young

Some animal parents carry their young. A kangaroo carries its baby in a pouch. A koala may carry its baby on its back.

Can you find the **12** objects in this Hidden Pictures puzzle?

snake

sock

hourglass

comb

teacup

boomerang

shoe

cane

canoe

crown

cotton swab

crescent moon

TALK ABOUT IT!

Why do you think some animal parents carry their young? How might that help the young survive?

Animals Feed Their Young

Many animal parents feed their young. Read the text below. Find out how one baby bird gets a worm for dinner.

Look at the baby. It opens its beak to show it is hungry. *Chirp, chirp!*

Mom finds a worm to bring to the nest.

Mom drops the worm in her baby's beak. *Gulp!*

TALK ABOUT IT!

• What does the baby bird do to show it is hungry? What do you do and say when you are hungry?

• How is the mother bird helping her baby stay alive?

Can you help this bird get dinner to her hungry babies?

START

FINISH

Young and Parent Plants

This seedling starts out small. Over time, it will grow much bigger. One day it will tower over people.

spruce tree seedling

adult spruce tree

Parent plants make new plants. A young plant may look different from its parents. It will grow and change.

Look at each young plant and its parent plant. Circle the parts on the parent plant that are different.

Young Plant	Parent Plant
young pumpkin plant	parent pumpkin plant
young bean plant	parent bean plant

TALK ABOUT IT!

• How are each young plant and its parent plant alike? How are they different?

• What does the parent plant have that the young plant does not?

Go Garden!

Number the pictures 1–4 to show how a tomato plant grows.

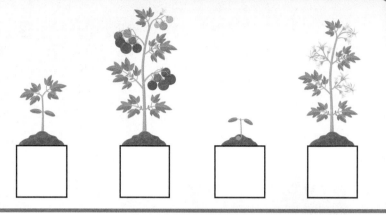

There are **6** words (not pictures!) hidden in the scene below. Can you find BLOOM, DIG, FARM, GARDEN, SEED, and VINE?

Circle the tomato plants in the scene.

TALK ABOUT IT!
- How does a tomato plant change as it grows?
- What other plants do you see in the picture? What might the young of each plant look like?

Animals of the Same Kind

These kittens are all brothers and sisters. But they do not look exactly the same.

How many kittens are orange and white? How many are black and orange and white?

TALK ABOUT IT!

Think about your traits. How tall are you? What color hair and eyes do you have? Compare your traits to those of your family members.

Find these **5** jigsaw pieces in this photo of fish. How are the fish alike? How are they different?

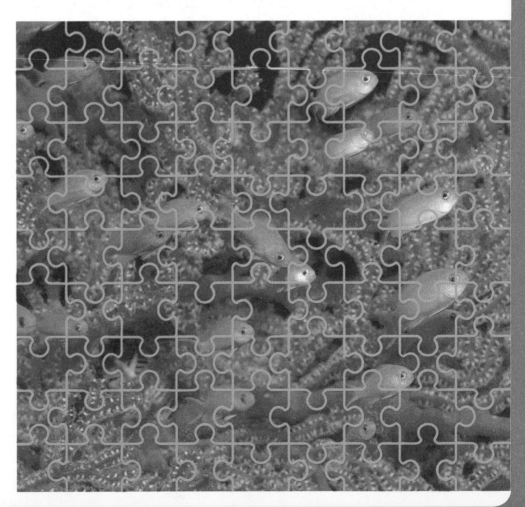

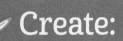 Create:
A Ladybug Snack

YOU NEED:

- apple • toothpicks • licorice laces • nut butter or sun butter
- raisins or chocolate chips • 2 grapes

1. Wash your hands.
2. Ask an adult to cut an apple in half and take out the seeds.
3. Use a toothpick to make 3 holes on each side of the apple halves (for the legs).
4. Put licorice pieces into the leg holes.
5. Place a piece of licorice down the middle of each apple half to make wings.
6. Dip a toothpick into the nut (or sun) butter. Dab each wing with the number of spots you want. Use a different number of spots for each apple half.
7. Press a raisin or chocolate chip into each dab of nut (or sun) butter.
8. For a head, use a toothpick to attach a grape to each apple half.
9. Enjoy eating your creation. Be careful not to eat the toothpick.

Ladybugs' spots are not all the same. Some have more spots than others. The spots can be different sizes and have different patterns.

TALK ABOUT IT!

- Look at the ladybugs in the photo. How are they the same? How are they different?
- How many spots did you put on each ladybug snack? How many spots did you make in all?

Leaves of the Same Kind

Look at the bunches of leaves on the left. Draw a line from each bunch on the left to the leaf on the right that could be from the same plant.

 ○   ○

 ○   ○

 ○   ○

TALK ABOUT IT!

Look at leaves from the same plant. Are they all the same shape? Do they differ in size? What color are they?

🔍 **Investigate:** Look for leaves in your neighborhood or a local park. Tell which ones are the same kind. Pick up leaves from the ground. Glue them onto paper to make a nature scene.

Create:
Paper Marigolds

These flowers are all marigolds, but they do not look exactly the same. What differences do you see?

 Make your own tissue-paper marigolds!

YOU NEED:
- **red, yellow, and orange tissue paper** • **green chenille sticks** • **scissors**

1. Fold the tissue paper like an accordion into 1-inch sections.
2. Fold the chenille stick in half around the folded tissue paper. Twist the 2 halves of the chenille stem together.
3. Cut off the corners of the tissue paper to make a point at each end.
4. Pull the tissue paper open one layer at a time.

TALK ABOUT IT!
- Tell about the flowers you made. Talk about the parts of your flowers.
- What could you do to make marigolds that are different sizes?

The Sun

The sun is Earth's closest star. It shines because it is so hot. The sun gives Earth light and heat.

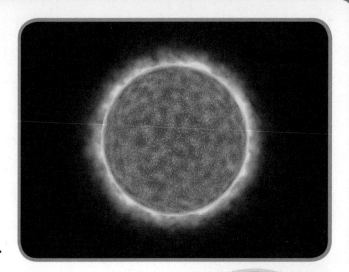

What do you like to do on a warm, sunny day? Draw a picture of it. Be sure to show the sun in your picture.

Remember: it's not safe to look directly at the sun.

TALK ABOUT IT!

• What does the sun look like from Earth?

• At what times of day can you see the sun in the sky?

• Think about the things you like to do outside during the day. Why might they be hard to do outside at night?

Day and Night

You can often see the sun in the daytime. You cannot see the sun at night.

Circle the picture of daytime. Draw a rectangle around the picture of nighttime.

TALK ABOUT IT!
- How could you tell which photo shows daytime and which one shows nighttime?
- What do the buildings look like at night?

Does this scene show day or night? Tell how you know. Then find the **8** objects in this Hidden Pictures puzzle.

mitten

envelope

arrow

boot

trowel

knitted hat

artist's brush

toothbrush

Stars at Night

People can use the pattern of stars in the sky to find their way.

Think about the night sky full of twinkling stars. The stars in the sky are always there. But we can see them only at night. It is too bright during the day to see them.

Find the Big Dipper.

Identify the two pointer stars. Draw an imaginary line between them.

Extend the line upward. The first bright star you come to is the North Star, also known as Polaris.

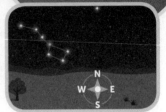

If you are facing the North Star, then north is in front of you, south is behind you, east is on your right, and west is on your left.

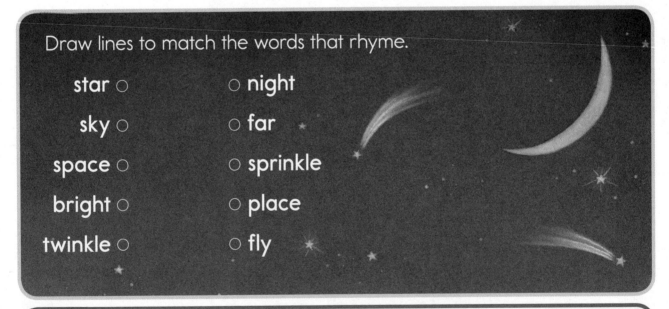

Draw lines to match the words that rhyme.

star ○   ○ night

sky ○   ○ far

space ○   ○ sprinkle

bright ○   ○ place

twinkle ○   ○ fly

TALK ABOUT IT!
- Why is it hard to see stars when the sky is cloudy?
- Where would you probably see more stars: in a busy city or in a field in the country? Why?

Investigate:
Patterns in the Sky

 How does the moon appear to change each day?

Each day for a week, look for the moon. When can you see the moon? What does it look like? Does it always look the same? Make the sky journal below to record your observations. Draw pictures and write about what you see. Write the date and time for each picture.

When you can see the whole moon, it is a full moon.

✂ Make a Sky Journal!

YOU NEED:

- hole punch
- 2 craft-foam sheets (5 inches by 8 inches)
- 10 to 15 index cards (5 inches by 8 inches)
- binder ring
- foam stickers or markers

1. Punch a hole in the corner of 2 sheets of craft foam and 10 to 15 index cards.

2. Put the index cards between the foam covers. Put a binder ring through the holes.

3. Decorate the cover of your journal with stickers or markers.

TALK ABOUT IT!

How did the shape of the moon seem to change?

Sunrise and Sunset

Remember, the sun does not move. It's Earth that is moving.

Wake up, sun! The sun **rises** in the morning. During the day, the sun appears to move across the sky. In the evening, the sun **sets**. Then, it is nighttime again.

Read the poem about sunrise.

Dawn breaks
wakes
turns the night
into drops
of dew
that drip
drip
drip
from the tip
tip
tips
of swaying
blades
of morning
grass
that dance
in the glow
of the sudden
sudden
sun.
—Charles Ghigna

Two of these pictures show a sunrise. Circle them.

TALK ABOUT IT!

• Have you ever seen a sunrise or sunset? What colors did you see?

• The amount of daylight differs from season to season. Think about dinnertime in the summer and dinnertime in the winter. When would you still see daylight? When would it be dark?

Inventions Everywhere

People create **inventions** to solve problems. First, inventors think about possible solutions for problems. Then they design an invention. They test it out many times until it is just right.

Look around you. Draw some of the everyday inventions that you see. We did one to get you started.

The steps you follow to invent something are called the engineering design process.

TALK ABOUT IT!

• Which of the inventions that you drew have you used today?

• What problem does each invention solve?

• Ask friends and family members what problems they would like to solve with new inventions.

 Invent:

An Ice Cube Saver

What can you make to stop ice cubes from melting too quickly?

Imagine you put ice cubes in a glass of lemonade. The ice melts and cools the lemonade. But as the ice melts, the lemonade gets watery. Can you invent something that will keep the ice from melting so fast?

Ice cubes are frozen water. Water freezes at 32 degrees Fahrenheit.

STEP 1: ASK QUESTIONS

Ask friends and family members if they know how other people have tried to solve this problem.

STEP 2: DESIGN A SOLUTION

Draw a design of the invention you would like to make.

STEP 3: MAKE A MODEL

Follow your plan to make your invention.

YOU NEED:

- 1 small cup of ice cubes
- fabric, bubble wrap, or other materials you want to use

STEP 4: ASK QUESTIONS

1. Put your invention (with the ice cubes) next to a second small cup of ice cubes.

2. Check the ice in both cups every 10 minutes. What happens? Which ice cubes melted sooner?

STEP 5: EVALUATE AND REDESIGN

- How well did your invention work?
- What could you change to make the ice cubes last even longer?
- Try out different designs and materials and compare the results.

TALK ABOUT IT!

- Do you think ice cubes will melt if you put them in the refrigerator? Why or why not?
- What happens to hot foods when you leave them out for a while? How could you keep hot foods hot?

Highlights

FIRST GRADE 1

Congratulations!

_____
(your name)

worked hard
and finished the
Hands-On
STEAM
Learning Fun Workbook

Glossary

beak part of a bird that helps it eat its food

engineering design process the steps you follow to invent something

flower the plant part that makes seeds

fruit the plant part that holds seeds

invention something that solves a problem

leaf the flat, green part of the plant that takes in sunlight

light energy that lets you see

mimic copy

opaque allows no light to pass through

predators animals that eat other animals

reflect to bounce back off a surface, as light does

roots the plant parts that take in water from the soil

seed the plant part from which a new plant grows

shadow what is made when an object blocks light

sound a kind of energy made by vibrations

sound waves how sound travels; can make objects vibrate

stem the plant part that moves water up from the roots to other parts of the plant

sun the star that's closest to Earth; it gives Earth light and heat

sunrise when the sun seems to appear in the sky in the morning

sunset when the sun seems to disappear from the sky in the evening

translucent allows some light to pass through

transparent allows all light to pass through

vibrations quick movements back and forth

Answers

Page 3
Quiet or Loud

Page 6
What is Light?

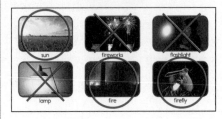

Page 8
Shadow Play

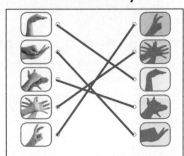

Pages 12–13
Devices From Here to There

Page 16
Animal Eyes

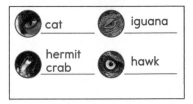

Page 17
Animal Safety

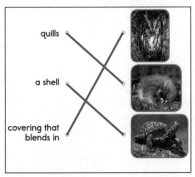

Page 22
Ideas from Nature

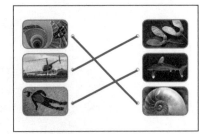

Page 25
Adult and Young Animals

Answers

Page 26
Animal Babies

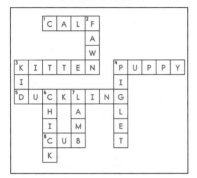

Page 28
Protecting Their Young

Page 29
Animals Feed Their Young

Page 31
Go Garden!

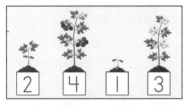

Page 32
Animals of the Same Kind

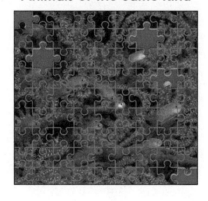

Page 34
Leaves of the Same Kind

Page 37
Day and Night

Page 38
Stars at Night

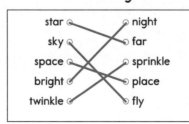

star — fly
sky — far
space — night
bright — sprinkle
twinkle — place

Page 40
Sunrise and Sunset

Extend the Learning

Want to explore further? Encourage your child's interest and curiosity in the topics throughout the book. Here are some ideas to get you started.

Sound *(pages 2–5; 14)*

Volume (loud or soft) and pitch (high or low) are two ways to describe sound. Go on a sound hunt with your child. Use a smartphone to record interesting sounds both inside and outside of your home. Talk about the volume and pitch of each sound. Then encourage your child to create a sound song with noises other than his voice.

Light *(pages 6–13; 15)*

On a sunny day, go outside with your child to observe shadows. Bring along some chalk. After you find interesting shadows in your environment, have your child stand in a sunny place on a driveway or sidewalk. Trace her shadow. Return later in the day and trace her shadow again. Discuss: *What do you notice? How has the shadow changed? Why has it changed?*

Animals and Their Parts *(pages 16–19)*

Work with your child to observe and draw pets and other animals, such as birds, squirrels, fish, and insects, that live nearby. Compare the parts of the animals in the drawings. Ask: *Do all the animals have eyes, mouths, feet, and so on? Which animals have different parts, such as wings, tails, and fins? How does each part help an animal get what it needs to live?* Extend the learning by comparing animal parts with the parts of people. Ask: *How are they alike and different? How do our parts help us get what we need to live?*

Plants and Their Parts *(pages 20–21)*

Use the diagram of plant parts on page 20 to aid you and your child in identifying the parts of plants in your home, yard, and neighborhood. Discuss how the parts differ on different plants.